A CONNOISSEUR'S
GUIDE TO ANTIQUE
DOLLS

A CONNOISSEUR'S GUIDE TO ANTIQUE

DOLLS

RONALD PEARSALL

TODTRI

This book was designed and produced by TODTRI Book Publishers
P.O. Box 572, New York, NY 10116-0572
Fax: (212) 695-6984
e-mail: todtri@mindspring.com

Printed and bound in Singapore

ISBN 1-57717-150-0

Visit us on the web!
www.todtri.com

Author: Sally Taylor

Publisher: Robert M. Tod
Editor: Nicolas Wright
Art Directorr: Ron Pickless
Typesetting & DTP: Blanc Verso UK

CONTENTS

INTRODUCTION

The recorded history of dolls begins in ancient Egypt. In fact several Egyptian dolls still survive, including one with a wooden head, rag body, and flexible arms, excavated from a site near Antenore. The cruder dolls were of clay, wood, or bone, but fine dolls were made from ivory, wax, fabric or terra cotta. It is certain that dolls existed long before then as they serve a deep-rooted instinct. It might be supposed that this is an early manifestation of the maternal instinct in young children, but some doll historians have disputed this, especially as dolls are not always identified as models of children. During the eighteenth century dolls were almost exclusively adults.

The early story of dolls is intriguing, for what appear to be dolls can be nothing of the kind; they can be idols, magical figurines, costume figures, and religious offerings, sometimes sacrificed to a god or buried in a tomb with the owner. This was particularly common in the ancient civilizations where they can be construed as servant substitutes to help in the afterlife.

The word "doll" itself is curious. It could be a corruption of "idol" or it could be derived from the name Dorothy (Dolly being a familiar shorted form). Again it could be a version of the Norse word *doul* meaning woman. The name was not known until well after the Middle Ages, "children's babies" or an equivalent being used.

Although dolls have long been considered children's playthings, there are some dolls which are so exquisite that they are far more than mere toys. They are, instead, works of art, eagerly sought after by collectors and treasured as family heirlooms. If and when such dolls - from whatever period - appear at auction they command often startlingly high prices.

This is the story of dolls through the ages, from primitive examples made from base material right through to the beautifully constructed china and wax dolls of the 18th century and later.

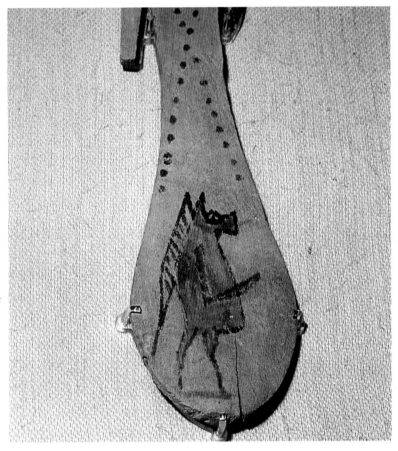

Above: An Egyptian doll of about 1900 BC. Egyptian dolls were the most sophisticated of the time, and although most were made of mundane materials such as terracotta some were made of rare and exotic precious stones and minerals.

Opposite: Two Hopi dolls from North America. It is often difficult to determine whether early dolls were playthings or whether they were elements in religious ceremonies and rites.

7

EARLY DOLLS

During the eighteenth, nineteenth and twentieth centuries excavations uncovered hundreds of small figures. Certain types of figures which were certainly dolls, and there is evidence from literature that in ancient Rome girls gave up their dolls to Venus when they married. This seems to imply that dolls were cherished until puberty, though the traditional peak interest in dolls is when the owner is between eight and ten. Until the beginning of this century, the ratio of female dolls to male dolls was twelve to one and there is no reason to believe that this has changed.

The oldest examples from Greece are terracotta pottery dolls with long legs and tiny arms but even as early as this there was an interest in giving dolls moving parts attached with wires. They have dresses painted with birds and geometrical motifs. Many dolls from the sixth century BC have movable arms and by the fifth century BC legs were attached at the knees. A curious feature of dolls of this time is that many hold cymbals. Dolls were often undressed, so presumably they were clothed by their owners.

By the fourth century BC legs were hollow and made with knee joints, with the legs being more efficiently inserted rather than suspended loosely on wires. Some dolls have holes in their heads and it is probably that string was passed through these and attached to the limbs so that they could be used as puppets. The models of these dolls seem to have been Greek dancing girls with pleated skirts.

The dolls of ancient Rome were increasingly sophisticated, and it is probable that they were of a quality that was not matched until the seventeenth century and later. In the coffin of a 14 year-old girl a 30 cm tall wooden doll was discovered with jointed shoulders, hips, elbows and knees. Bone was often used, and so was cloth and leather, but examples of these discovered in catacombs and the like have deteriorated and rotted so much that it is difficult to assess them. Some were certainly crude, probably home made. Ivory dolls of high quality were also discovered in catacombs (some on display in the Vatican Museum), with the limbs secured with small pins, and the condition of these is often excellent, so that it is possible to see that the dolls' hair styles were in line with current fashion.

Because of the haphazard discovery of ancient dolls it is not possible to do any more more than sketch in the systematic history. It is obvious, however, that dolls increased in sophistication.

Above: An Egyptian bone doll dating from between the ninth and twelfth century AD, long after the great days of Egypt had passed

Opposite: A wax doll reputed to date from 1641. Later Britain became pre-eminent in wax dolls, which had a warmth and a lustre that was inclined to be lacking in the more formalistic china dolls, in which the French and later the Germans led. Because of the vulnerability of wax, the survival rate is not high.

Left: Peruvian wood and fabric "grave" dolls of indeterminate age, though this description is open to question as burial customs of South America remain largely unknown.

Some have been found accompanied by miniature pots and a doll's wine service. In fourth-century BC Athens a young woman was buried with a terracotta doll seated in a chair holding a dove with accompanying shoes, a spinning apparatus and a bowl on a stand. It has been suggested that she was probably a young bride.

As with all types of toys, the children of the great civilizations of the past formally took leave of their dolls when they reached puberty, though it is probable that many were retained by those girls who remained single, as is the case today, as substitute children. The top-quality dolls of the eighteenth and especially the nineteenth century were intended for women.

Because of the systematic excavations in Egypt, Greece and Rome far more is known of classical dolls than dolls elsewhere, though it is known that dolls were in use among the Arabs at the time of Mohammed (c570 – 632). Even though Islam forbids the representation of the human figure, obviously exceptions were allowed, and the prophet's nine-year-old wife Ayesha is said to have persuaded him to join her in playing with them.

Above: A German mourning doll of 1901, a rare genus as dolls were made to give joy rather than as reminders of death.

Opposite: Wood and papier mâché doll. Papier mâché was often used by itself or with other materials. It had proved the ideal, as it was robust, cheap and the makers did not need the technical expertise of the china doll makers.

Dolls were common in Africa, though it is difficult to say whether they were playthings or have a magical significance. Some were known as "stool children" and were placed on a stool at home, the reason for which must always remain mysterious. Australian Aborigine children had dolls made of cane, but these probably had some magical properties, which was possibly true of the figurines discovered by the Spaniards in Mexico and South America.

With the fall of the Roman Empire details of dolls are sparse and inconclusive. Life was short, nasty and brutish, though unquestionably dolls or doll substitutes played a part in the growing up of a

Above: Two North American Indian dolls of the mid-nineteenth century when European influences were beginning to make themselves felt amongst the native Americans.

Opposite: A French blue cotton dress of about 1867. Many dolls were sold without clothes so that the young owner could dress them themselves, but for the rich where price was no object high fashion was copied in miniature including numerous accessories.

child. With the abandonment of ritual burial except on rare occasions (such as the celebrated Sutton Hoo ship burial in England), there is little trace of specimens. Commonsense tells us that crude rag or carved wooden dolls were used. In later years we know that peasants in the long winter evenings carved wooden dolls and went around from door to door selling them and there is no reason to suppose that this was not a long-established practice.

There is almost no history of rag dolls, or whether these were made for pedlars to sell or whether they were made by mothers or sisters for the children. What we do know is that they were greatly treasured and handed down from one generation to another until they disintegrated. There is little literature on them though we see them in pictures and they feature frequently in satirical magazine cartoons by artists such as John Leech in the Victorian period. They were unquestionably made from any material that was handy, surplus material from homemade clothes and as the population was mostly rural farm animals would provide the stuffing of wool and horse hair.

Quality would vary enormously, and in the eighteenth and nineteenth centuries seamstresses and dressmakers who were often outworkers must have produced fine examples, though, from the specimens that have been garnered by enterprising collectors, most were rough and ready. Eyes were often buttons, and the features were crudely sketched in with beet or fruit juices. Many rag dolls have layers of faces, indicating that when one wore out a fresh one was sewn on. Crude wigs of yarn or hemp were used, though some had human hair.

Superior rag dolls were shown at the Great Exhibition of 1851at Alexandra Palace in England, but the adjudicators were sniffy about them, though praising the elaborate costumes, and rag dolls were made commercially throughout the century. There were many patents for rag dolls in America in the early twentieth century, especially cut-out designs to be made in the home.

Legends about dolls are all that survives from medieval times, though a clay woman and baby in fourteenth-century costume were

found under a Nuremburg paving stone in Germany. It is said that dolls of wood, wax and papier mâché were shown at annual fairs in Florence and Venice in the fourteenth century. Documents of the fifteenth century include the records of Nuremburg doll-makers, and there are woodcuts showing doll-makers at work, though there is little evidence of what the dolls actually looked like until they began to appear in contemporary paintings. In a Vienna museum is a doll reputed to be of the sixteenth century.

In the seventeenth century dolls were made mainly of wood and wax, though some heads were made of pottery, and there is reference to dolls being made in gold, silver, and alabaster, though, again, it is difficult to say whether these are dolls as playthings or miniature figures as objets d'art. In 1700 a wax baby doll which is alleged to have cried and turned its eyes was bought for five shillings (25p) in England, so there is evidence of great sophistication which seems to have been lost. In 1737 walking dolls were made in Paris, though how successful they were is open to doubt as it was only in the late nineteenth century that the prob-

lem was solved, and a true walking doll was created rather than a walking-and-falling-over doll.

Dolls pre-1750 are rare and difficult to date, especially if they are wooden and crudely carved by amateurs. Those early wooden dolls of quality which do exist and survive against all the odds are more than likely not playthings but crèche dolls which were religious figures made to take part in Nativity tableaux and other events in the Christian calendar. Some dolls end up in museums, and tradition decrees that they be treated with some awe but mostly they are artistically pathetic and any real interest lies in the costume in which they are dressed.

This is especially true of pedlar dolls, where not only the clothes are of prime importance but also the accessories, which could consist of barrows of fruit, trays of knickknacks, wicker baskets of clothes, any-

Above: An old woman character doll, made of felt and cotton and stuffed with straw.

Previous pages: A doll's tea party automaton of about 1900, an area in which the French and Swiss were supreme.

Opposite: A Chinese-featured doll with bisque head socketed into a composition body made by the German firm of Bahr and Proschild about 1890, a time when the French were yielding premier place because of the greater efficiency of the Germans.

thing in fact which an itinerant pedlar was likely to sell. They were largely parlour exhibits and were usually kept under glass domes to keep dust away and prevent them being appropriated by children. They were made mostly in the nineteenth century and it was a favourite hobby for women. The usual costuming for a woman pedlar was a shawl and apron, with a brown or black bonnet and a cape, while the men could be attired in anything, from peasants' smocks to jackets and stove-pipe hats. The genuine pedlar doll was any spare doll, perhaps the worse for wear, that was handy at the time. The faces are very rarely good looking and ugliness was often emphasised, which would suggest that many were commercially made as ugly dolls have no sales appeal. Pedlars or hawkers were regarded with some suspicion and fear. They were inclined to steal anything that was not nailed down, and the wives – for pedlar dolls usually come in pairs – had a reputation for telling fortunes.

Many of the items found on the trays of pedlars were dolls' house accessories produced in quantity in Germany. Some pedlar dolls stand behind low tables, and some of these tables are equipped with awnings, and almost all pedlar dolls are of country origin. City pedlars are rare. Pedlar dolls are very much faked, as it is easy to surround a nondescript doll of low value with authentic-looking odds and ends, though sometimes the faker comes unstuck by including reels of cotton, when cotton was still sold in skeins.

WOODEN DOLLS

hroughout the millennia the most popular material for making dolls has been wood. Dolls made of wood vary from chunky objects in which it is difficult to detect any resemblance to any living thing and the most beautifully carved figures with finely painted faces, often of well known people of the time. The heads are the most important part of a doll; even where the heads are of the highest quality the rest of the body can be crude, with the limbs loosely pinned or wired. This did not matter very much to the owners, as their main aim was to dress it in as many different costumes as possible and the appeal (and value) of old dolls often lies in the sort of dress in which they are attired.

It possibly says something about the innate impatience of Queen Victoria that as a child she had 132 dolls, of which she dressed 32 – her governess did the others. Queen Victoria's dolls were mostly of the traditional wooden kind. In 1894 Francis Low wrote a book called Victoria's Dolls and commented that "the dolls are of the most unpromising material and would be regarded with scorn by the average Board School child of today, whose toys, thanks to modern philanthropists, are often of the most extravagant and expensive description", which tells us as much about Mr Low as about Victoria's dolls.

Many of the eighteenth-century wooden dolls when the art was at its peak are known as Queen Anne dolls, though there is little reason for this as she reigned for only a few years and the dolls of the first half of the eighteenth century have a strong family resemblance, and indeed there was little different in the dolls of the last half.

The best wooden dolls of the later eighteenth century come from

German pedlar doll with accessories, with composition head and "peg" body. These were often carved by peasants during the winter and sold at fairs and markets. The accessories and costume were often as important as the doll.

Opposite: The two most famous dolls in the world, Lord and Lady Clapham, made in wood between about 1690 and 1700, and surprisingly rare survivals.

Left: Lord and Lady Clapham. It would be interesting to know why they are so named. Until the late-nineteenth century dolls were anonymous; if they were playthings they had no need for a name.

A CONNOISSEUR'S GUIDE TO ANTIQUE
DOLLS

Below: English doll of about 1780, with a wooden body, linen arms, and a wig made from human hair. In fine dolls, human hair was fed into the scalp a strand at a time. In France doll makers as well as dress makers were a long-suffering class.

the cuckoo-clock area of Germany, where there was a tradition of superb carving of crèche figures for religious ceremonies, a craft easily adapted for secular purposes, and the faces and hands are particularly well delineated . Hands were long a problem for the less-skilled doll-makers, sometimes resembling scoops or forks.

In Britain the heads of wooden dolls of the first half of the eighteenth century are invariably out of proportion to the rest of the body, understandable as it was the most important part and gave more

scope to the painter. The features were usually painted to a formula, with thin pursed lips, rouged cheeks, and large eyes. Gesso (plaster of Paris) was often applied to the head before the paint was applied. The eyes were usually painted but sometimes glass eyes were inserted, and a fine George II doll c 1710-1735 had black glass eyes without pupils. These gave the dolls what has been described graphically as a pug-like appearance. This particular doll sold at auction in 1989 for £38,000.

German dolls had carefully carved hair styles but wigs, often made from human hair, were more common in Britain. These wigs were often interchangeable, and the bald heads frequently had a dot placed so that the doll's owner would know where to position the wig. An interesting characteristic of eighteenth-century dolls is the use of arched eyebrows giving almost all dolls a petulant look. Beauty spots were sometimes applied. The lips are always closed, and the open mouth had to wait until the end of the nineteenth century. This was a technical problem only solved when fine china was used for dolls' heads.

Perhaps the most famous wooden dolls are "Lord and Lady Clapham", dating from about 1690, who found a home in the Victoria and Albert Museum, London, after being

26

sold at auction in 1974 for £16,000. They are opulently clothed in period costume and seated on curious deformed chairs and completely expressionless. This was was the case with most dolls throughout the eighteenth and well into the nineteenth centuries, which reflects badly on British doll-making when the German wooden dolls are anatomically perfect, often resembling artists' lay figures. Invariably the neck of an English doll is round and elongated and stuck on top of the torso rather than being set into the body.

Fashion was becoming increasingly more important, and émigré Huguenot silk workers in Spitalfields in London brought a version of *haute couture* to the British. Dolls were provided with a variety of immaculate and superbly made costumes. A doll with several outfits and accessories including a fan said to have been owned by Marie Antoinette while she was imprisoned in the Tuileries is in the collection of the Wiltshire and Blackmore Museum in America. The most famous doll in America is "Old Susan" dating from about 1690 which is in the Museum of the City of New York, though dolls were amongst the trinkets brought to America in 1585 to trade with the native Americans.

Towards the end of the eighteenth century the stereotyped wooden doll was under competition from wax dolls, a field in which Britain was predominant, but many thoughtful parents still preferred the wooden doll as being more amenable to rough treatment. The wooden dolls were becoming more sophisticated with ball-jointed limbs, though there was an increasing demand for cheap dolls for the mass market. Although limb parts in the eighteenth century could be made of leather or other material to add flexibility, later doll-makers dispensed with articulated limbs and instead used dangling tubes of leather or fabric filled with sawdust. The

Carved wooden German doll of about 1825, probably originating in the Black Forest area which long had a reputation for carving and which eventually produced the most popular carved object in use today, the cuckoo clock.

Above: A hooded pedlar doll of the 1860 - 1870 period.

Opposite: The ratio of male to female dolls is about one in twelve, except with pedlar dolls where male figures with the tools of their trade score more highly. The date for this doll is given as 1830, and the head is made of kid leather.

heads of these cheap dolls were carved and shaped with the minimum of fuss and are known as the "bedpost" type. Flounced skirts reaching the ground meant that some doll-makers rejected legs complete-ly and instead used a circular frame to support the skirt.

The flounced skirts of the eighteenth century gave way to the more natural costume of the Regency period (1811 – 1826), and this necessitated a change of shape to the dolls, cutting down on the extra-wide hips which helped to hold the skirt up. It is custom-ary to call most nineteenth-century wooden dolls Dutch dolls as a term of disparage-ment This is misleading as the Dutch were not involved in large-scale export (and the word Dutch may be a corrup-tion of Deutch (German)) until towards the end of the century. But the introduction of German wooden dolls known as Grödnertals, from the area of Germany where they origi-nated, eclipsed the British dolls. Grödnertals are charac-terised by slim high-waisted bodies, hair made of plaited cord and painted, and framing the face with short curls, as well as being equipped with flat-heeled painted slippers and a reasonably sized head. Heads were still often without ears, but earrings were sometimes screwed directly into the head.

Grödnertals were cheaper than their equivalent English dolls, made of softwood, with pivoted or ball-jointed limbs. The lower arms and legs were painted but the torso left plain. They varied in size from half an inch (1.3 cm) to 40 inch (101 cm), and the larger ones have a swivel joint at the waist, but the big demand from Britain and America led to a slight falling off in quality and about 1830 they began to decline in popularity.

In eighteenth century Germany Guild rules had dictated that the painting was done by dedicated craftsmen, but these fell into disuse,

Above: A significant achievement - Queen Victoria in her coronation robes. The head and arms are of wax, the body wood and fabric. It was made by the renowned wax-doll makers the Pierotti family, Italian immigrants.

and there was a consequent variation in the quality. The artists of the Oberammergau area were reckoned to be the most skilled and dolls from all over Germany were sent there for completion. The paint was water based and protected by varnish, which gave a warm quality, unlike the cold finish imparted by gloss paint used in the late nineteenth century. Male Grödnertal figures are rare, and most are tiny, intended for dolls' houses.

Poorer children were presented with stick-like figures carved in one piece to resemble swaddling babies or Tauflinge, made in quantity in Germany, crudely carved but made acceptable by the brilliant colour of the blankets in which they were placed. These maintained their popularity on the continent until World War I but had a limited appeal to British or American children. It is often difficult to assign the place of origin to some dolls; the Essex Institute in Salem, Massachusetts, holds an interesting group of dolls where the stick legs fit directly onto square bases. They are dressed in French Empire style and are believed to be French. The square base was a logical solution to the problem of keeping dolls standing up, and perhaps indicate that some opulently dressed dolls were not intended to be played with but were ornaments. Certainly few wooden dolls, whatever their provenance, can have been cuddly; that was the province of rag dolls.

Dolls make an appearance in many genre paintings of the nineteenth century, one of best examples being Thomas Webster's Returning from the Fair of 1837 where a young girl is proudly holding up for her grandmother to see a Grödnertal doll dressed in green and red. A Grödnertal was the quintessential nineteenth-century wooden doll, and no doubt was copied by unknown English doll-makers. There was some variation; there was sometimes a coating of wax over the paint to add realism.

Although wooden dolls continued to be made for the poor throughout the nineteenth century, and were sold at fairs, bazaars and by travelling pedlars and street traders, palatial arcades and shops catered for the better off and promoted the more sophisticated and expensive composition and china dolls. In 1895 that there was a revival of interest amongst the richer toy-buying public for more primitive dolls when Florence Upton of New York wrote a book nar-

Below: A Russian ethnic doll of the late-nineteenth century. The Russians are mainly known for their sets of dolls in diminishing sizes which fit into each other, curiously has never been copied elsewhere.

rating the adventures of two wooden peg dolls and a Golliwog, which she had invented. Peg dolls were once again in fashion, imported in quantity from Holland and Germany, skittle-shaped and crude, with rudimentary painting on the face while the hair was no longer carved or in the form of wigs but a daub of black paint. It was as though history was reversing itself, but it is clear that gaily coloured wood dolls were ephemeral novelties in the fast-changing world of the 1890s and would soon be replaced by something else.

The only new path was explored by an American toymaker, Albert Schoenhut, of German descent. In 1872 he opened a factory in Philadelphia to counter the import of German toys and dolls, but it was not until 1909 that he patented the first spring-jointed wooden doll, a step towards dolls, and, especially, toys and animals where the limbs and other extensions could be stretched in any direction and remain there. Schoenhut's dolls were not especially attractive. Thick enamel paint was used for painting the face, which quickly crazed and flaked.

The Americans began to

Above: Crude painted wood late-nineteenth-century German dolls.

build up their own doll industry from the 1850s. The first patent for a doll's head was registered by Ludwig Greiner of Philadelphia, described as a "toy-man" in 1858, though it was for a composition head of paper, whiting, rye flour and glue, reinforced with linen and muslin. There was no apparent interest in jointed wooden dolls until 1873 when Joel Ellis of the Co-operative Manufacturing Company evolved a superior mode of jointing which enabled the dolls to adopt various postures and have the rare ability to stand up. In style they were heavier and more clumsy than equivalent German dolls. Maple wood was used for the dolls' bodies but the feet and hands were of metal.

Folksy gaily coloured wooden dolls such as the Russian dolls-in-a-set have continued to be made, but there is no pretence to present them as basic girls' dolls with the competition of dozens of other new and far more suitable and pliable materials.

Opposite: Unusually this legless wax doll by Pierotti is set on a wooden stick handle.

THE ADVENT OF WAX

All life responds to technical innovation, no matter how reluctantly – the sailing ship gave way to the steamship, the horse-drawn wagon to the train, the Hispano-Suiza to the Ferrari, the typewriter to the word processor – and this is evident in the manufacture of dolls. Skills gained in one field can be utilised in another one, especially true in the making of wax dolls where artists, whose job was to supply effigy figures of dead babies to grieving parents, could easily transfer their talents to the profitable doll market.

Wax had been used for dolls in the ancient civilizations, but have only survived under special circumstances, and examples from later civilizations are not common until the eighteenth century, a time when wax portrait busts were fashionable. A wax boy doll from a dolls' house of between 1691 and 1700 is in existence, especially interesting because it has a partly open mouth showing the tip of a tongue. German museums contain several wax dolls of the early eighteenth century. In 1722 Daniel Defoe, author of Robinson Crusoe, makes reference to a three foot wax doll presented to the young queen of France.

George IV of England (1762 – 1830) was modelled as a child, and his image lay on his mother's dressing table as a reminder of his brief innocence. Between 1773 and 1786 Thomas Engelhardt submitted a large number of wax portraits for exhibition at the London Royal Academy. Eighteenth-century wax dolls are

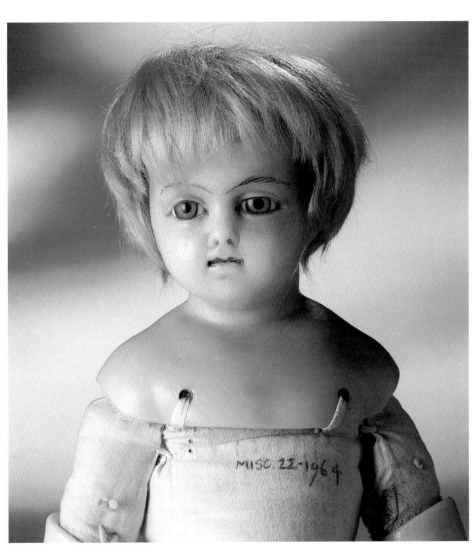

Above: Lucy Peck was a renowned English doll maker and her doll here doll has wax head and shoulders and a cloth body.

Opposite: A wax-headed mid-nineteenth century doll by Bazzoni. Dolls in wax were more labour-intensive than china dolls, and the high-quality dolls commanded very high prices.

uncommon, but there is a fine example dating from about 1757 in the Bethnal Green Museum, London, which has a naturalism lacking in wooden dolls of the period.

There are two kinds of wax dolls, those made in the solid, and those made by the poured wax method, which eventually became far more common. Although solid wax dolls of the highest quality were made in France and Germany by artists skilled in producing religious images, wax became an English speciality from the late eighteenth century. These are known as Pumpkin Heads, with the hair, head and bust moulded in one, with pupil-less brown glass eyes (brown eyes were replaced in the late 1830s by blue eyes when Queen Victoria ascended the throne).

Between the solid wax and poured wax dolls there was a hybrid, flourishing from about 1820, in which up to ten layers of wax were poured over painted papier mâché to produce a soft natural sheen. These dolls are known as Slitheads because of the slits in the head where the wigs were held in place. Holes were cut out for the eyes, which could often be manipulated by pulling wire or string through the body. Bodies were made of stuffed cotton or linen and less often kid. It is rare to find Slitheads in good condition as the applied wax crazed and faded badly.

Wax dolls reveal the doll-maker's skill at its highest. The extreme naturalism often unnerves collectors who prefer the prettier and more formalised china dolls of later years. Some time around 1840 poured wax dolls came into being, and were shown at the Great Exhibition of 1851. The artist modelled the bust in clay, and a plaster cast was taken, sometimes in several pieces. The moulds were then fixed together and molten wax poured in. After slight cooling the surplus was poured away, leaving a hardening layer. When this shell was cold another layer could be added. This method was suitable for arms and legs as well as the head. The mould could be of many materials including metal, and after it was removed the eye-sockets of the head were cut away. Sometimes the crown was removed so that the eyes could be more easily fitted in.

The bodies were often of stuffed cotton. Heads could be fitted up with wigs though the insertion of tufts of human hair or mohair was more common, the maker using a heated tool to press the hair in and smoothing away the damage to the wax with a heated roller. When the head was painted it was rubbed with talc or pumice to give a matt finish. For custom-made dolls, hair from the girl for whom the doll was intended could be used. The wax itself often had resin added to it to make it more amenable to treatment.

The poured-wax doll market was dominated by a handful of families, especially the Montanaris and the Pierottis. The Pierottis were making wax dolls from the 1780s in Britain. Domenico Pierotti came to England on a visit, and it is said that he had had such a bad channel crossing that he could not face a return journey, and so opened a doll-making firm. The Pierotti family supplied dolls to the famous toy shop Hamley's in Regent Street, London, well into the 1930s, and many of the original moulds were used which gave them an old-fashioned look. Henry Pierotti modelled many of his figures on his own daughters. Pierottis are characterised by soft features with heads turned slightly to one side, and the hair was usually mohair. They

DOLL
OVER 100 YEARS

Left: A wax and composition Taufling doll c 1860, a German Grodneraal doll in Welsh costume, a German papier-mâché doll of the mid-nineteenth century, and a wax-headed doll.

Overleaf: A doll representing a male court official in Rajpur, India, at the turn of the century. Simon and Halbig between about 1880 and 1890.

A CONNOISSEUR'S GUIDE TO ANTIQUE
DOLLS

Previous page: The Germans made their dolls into distinct characters rather than urbane Parisians and these character dolls are highly sought after. This one was made by Kammer and Reinhardt and

produced a quantity of male and religious figures. If there was a fault it was the too reddish tint of the cheeks.

Napoleon Montanari was born in Corsica in 1813, married an Englishwoman, and set up in business in Britain. It was Madame Augusta Montanari who won a prize medal for her poured-wax exhibits at the Great Exhibition of 1851. It was described as follows:

> The Display of this Exhibitor is the most remarkable and beautiful collection of toys in the Great Exhibition. It is a series of dolls representing all ages, from infancy to womanhood, arranged in several family groups... The dolls have hair, eyelashes and eyelids separately inserted in wax.... a variety of expressions are given to the figures in regard to the ages and stations which they were intended to represent. The dolls are adapted for children of the wealthy rather than general sale, undressed dolls sell from 10 shillings (50p), dressed dolls are much more expensive.

So expensive that Madame Montanari also displayed a small number of rag dolls aimed at the proletariat.

These families produced on a commercial scale, with the Pierotti dolls more numerous today, and it is surprising that the standard of portraiture is so high. One rare doll has a slightly open mouth, fitted out with china teeth. The Montanaris in particular produced portrait dolls of the queen both in youth and in old age (a difficult task as Queen Victoria was not without vanity). In general, Montanari dolls are heavier with a more pronounced waist than those of Pierotti. Few dolls were marked and the various members of the Montanari family were distributed throughout London. It is not known whether they worked separately or as a co-operative; nor is it definitely known whether dolls attributed to them were theirs or made by some unknown maker.

After 1887 Montanari was no longer listed as a doll-maker in the London Directory. Other major British doll-makers among the 16 doll-makers listed in the last quarter of the nineteenth century were Charles Marsh who not only made but cleaned and repaired wax dolls, Mrs Lucy Peck, H. J. Meech, supplier to the royal family, and the firm of W. H. Cremer & Son. Meech made a few dolls with sound boxes operated by pulling a string, and eyes were often fitted that could be opened and closed by pulling a string located in the body.

The kudos gained in the Great Exhibition did not last very long and poured wax was at its peak about 1860 – 1870 when cheaper composition dolls offered stern competition. In the 1860s wax masks were covered with muslin and these are known as "London Rag Dolls". Although poured wax dolls were realistic, they were not cuddly, being easily broken and in hot weather had a tendency to melt. One unfortunate wax doll melted while on display at the Paris Exhibition of 1876. There was little deterioration in quality until the end of the century. Wax had been replaced by a new medium not because it was necessarily better but because it was new.

Although wax is not over-fragile, it was not an ideal substance for the hard usage demanded by children, and it must be supposed that the children themselves preferred soft rag dolls. There is no doubt that the important doll-makers of the nineteenth century were as

Opposite: All dolls have their devotees though the china, wax, and bisque (unglazed porcelain) headed dolls are the most fervently sought. Papier-mâché dolls tend to be a poorer relation, though in quality they often match the others.

Left: *Three Brazilian dolls made of black cotton cloth, presumably for the home market as Brazil has no history of doll making.*

concerned with providing dolls for women as they were for children.

Throughout the nineteenth century wax had been combined with other materials, the most famous example being the Slitheads, but wood, porcelain, rag, rubber, and metal were all coated with wax. In 1887 a patent was given to an American doll-maker for a method in which a cloth head is dipped in wax.

Because of its unique warm quality, high-quality wax dolls were made well into the twentieth century in modest numbers, but they were also used especially in France and America as mannequins for display in shop windows or in tableaux. In 1925 in Paris a Madame Lazarski made wax dolls which were put on display in art galleries and were used in films. At the lower end of the market wax figures were used in waxwork museums, once a feature of many British seaside resorts.

Papier mâché was a doll-making material in its own right. Like wax, papier mâché ("chewed paper") was used from ancient times, though little has survived and it follows the discovery in China of papermaking. Known examples include a lacquered military helmet and pot-lids, the latter attributed to the Han Dynasty c AD 206. In the eighteenth century papier mâché was used for wall brackets, sconces, and mirror surrounds. The process was described in the eighteenth century as taking slips of brown paper then "boil them in Common Water and mash it with a stick while it boils. When it is almost a paste, take it from the Water and beat it well in a mortar til (sic) reduced to a pulp. Then make a strong Gum-Water with Gum-Arabick and Water, a quantity sufficient to cover your Paper-paste an inch. Put these together in a glazed Pipkin [a small pot] and let boil, stirring well til impregnated with the Gum. Put into mould." In later years other ingredients were added, and steam moulds were used from 1847.

Papier mâché was mainly used for furniture (including a piano) and trays, and also for pre-fabricated houses, and proved to be a strong versatile material. Although there are largely incomplete and battered papier-mâché dolls from the eighteenth century, it was used for dolls commercially from about 1810, supposedly introduced to Sonneberg a toy-making town in Germany from Paris about 1807. By 1820 papier mâché dolls were in full production with kid or wooden bodies and wooden legs, and they featured in the Great Exhibition of 1851. They were provided both with wigs and hair, and even bamboo teeth. As with wax dolls, they began to be in competition with the more sophisticated china dolls, but they were much cheaper to produce, and as the century progressed they were not much more expensive than wooden dolls. Around 1870 papier mâché was used for fully jointed dolls' bodies. The first American patent for a doll's head was registered in 1858 by Ludwig Greiner of Philadelphia, and this was papier mâché reinforced by strips of muslin over the joins .

These dolls were popular well into the twentieth century, but they were inclined to deteriorate, though, unlike the wax dolls, they were not eaten by children. Unless lacquered, as the furniture and trays were, papier mâché is apt to get "nibbled" and comes apart in flaky tufts. These distinctive dolls occupy a secondary place in the hierarchy. There are few museum-quality pieces, though they have an unmistakable charm.

Opposite: A Japanese doll of rather ungainly form dating from the turn of the century. Japan, except for copies of fine French and German dolls, had no creative impact on the toy market until the 1950s when they pioneered "technological" toys such as robots and space craft and introduced electronics into the industry.

DOLLS OF THE GRANDE EPOCH

Porcelain differs from pottery in that it is fired at a higher temperature, and is noted for its whiteness, thinness of body and translucency. The secrets were not known in the west, though imports of Chinese porcelain fostered intense experimentation. "Soft paste" porcelain was produced experimentally in Florence about 1575, but it was expensive and excessively fragile, and the factory only lasted ten years and it was not until the 1670s that soft paste porcelain was successfully produced in France. "Hard paste", true porcelain, was invented at Meissen (Dresden) about 1708, and although attempts were made to keep the processes secret they spread throughout the western world.

Some authorities declare that the earliest glazed porcelain (china) dolls were made about 1750, others that the year should be much later as surviving examples date from around the 1830s. After about 1845 they were made in vast quantities, and although they were more expensive than wooden dolls and rag dolls they were within the price range of the middle classes. They competed directly in the market place with wax dolls, which had the edge over porcelain in the naturalism that could be imparted to the complexion. Porcelain compared with wax was cold and hard. Some of the "dolls" are so elaborately dressed that they may well be couturiers' models.

Both porcelain and wax dolls were easily broken, but porcelain

Above: This is a bisque-headed googlie-eyed doll. The bulging eyes were a feature of many dolls and surprisingly did not detract from the appeal.

Opposite: Victorian china doll showing the layers of clothes.

Left: A child's gazebo made in Germany about 1870 and a fine quality doll by Kammer and Reinhardt, made at a time when the German dolls were as good as the French - though some experts cavil at this.

Above: Simon and Halbig is one of the major names in doll making. This one has a bisque (unglazed porcelain) head. Bisque-head dolls were often more finely modelled that their china counterparts, just as bisque figures made by Sevres have few rivals. The reason is technical; having no glaze, bisque could be more decisive and crisp.

Opposite: Victoria, a rare French doll of high quality. Towards the end of the nineteenth century there was a tendency to personalise dolls as the makers started to impart personality.

dolls had the advantage that they could be washed. Porcelain, as with wax, was used for the parts of the body that could be seen and, as part of the appeal of dolls is dressing and undressing them, the bodies were not considered important and were mostly of cotton, filled with sawdust or other substances. From the beginning it was clear that the Germans and the French were masters in the field, and it was not until the closing years of the century that the British and the Americans, especially the Americans who were adept at bringing novelty into a fairly staid area, made any major impression on the Franco-German monopoly.

China dolls came in an immense variety of styles, from the stylised and slightly stupid to the naturalistic. They also came in three different varieties of porcelain, often regarded by writers on dolls as if they were somehow distinct from each other. These are glazed china, unglazed china (bisque or biscuit), and Parian, a slightly glazed white porcelain imitating marble. Sometimes glazed and unglazed china was used in combination. The crowns of glazed heads were left unglazed so that the slightly matt surface would hold a wig better. Glazed china

dolls were immensely popular until about 1860 when bisque became favourite. Early examples of glazed china dolls have sloping shoulders, a faint red line over the eyelids and painted slippers, while later examples have button boots.

Curiously, the different types of porcelain resulted in different styles of doll. Parian dolls often represent haughty and superior women. Bisque and Parian were especially popular from the 1850s. Dolls' heads were often sold separately with the new owner entrusted to make some kind of body, and these dolls sometimes create confusion amongst collectors. Rose-tinted bisque was perhaps more realistic than hard glaze porcelain painting, but throughout the century there was a constant fluctuation in favourite colouring, hairstyles, and costume, which was usually contemporary but sometimes harked back to the eighteenth century. In the last quarter of the nineteenth century there was an increasing emphasis on child-like dolls, and more boys were made. Dolls were sometimes given moulded hats and bonnets.

Above: A French doll of about 1870. Even the finest dolls are often unsigned and then only by the manufacturer not the modeller, perhaps because each head went through a variety of hands and the modeller, unlike those who made fine porcelain figures, was not supreme.

The French supremacy in doll manufacture began in earnest about 1862, and the dolls of this period are known as Parisiennes. The earlier ones are noted for their chubby child-like features and a curious habit of dotting the nostrils with two red spots giving a somewhat pig-like appearance. The features are not particularly full of expression, but the dolls are invariably beautifully dressed, and often have a range of sophisticated accessories. These Parisiennes are known as "Rohmer types" after one of the predominant manufacturers who pioneered what is known as a "cup and saucer" swivelling joint for the neck.

Bisque was used instead of glazed china from about 1860, wigs were usually of sheepskin, and the bodies were not of cotton but leather, usually kid, though sometimes a metal or wooden frame was utilised over which the leather was stretched. Wooden bodies were occasionally used, and manufacturers were not afraid to experiment, both in the make-up of the torsos and in evolving new types of joint so that the doll could be tormented and twisted into different poses, the often cumbersome costumes permitting. Completely jointed wooden bodies enabled the dolls to be placed in various poses, including kneeling. The joints of the leather-bodied dolls were inclined to swell with sawdust, and the dolls too often assumed a strange crouching posture.

Although the sewing machine was well established, the costumes were more often handmade by hundreds of Parisian seamstresses, most of them outworkers and most of them starving. There was plenty of work for them and other outworkers; layettes for baby dolls could consist of ten items, and there were gloves, hats, shoes, fans, handbags, umbrellas, not to mention accessories such as hand-mirrors, hair brushes, even tea sets. The children of the rich were demanding; they insisted that their dolls were dressed in the latest styles and if the colour of the eyes was out of fashion the dolls were sent back to the manufacturer for fresh eyes to be inserted.

The two main names in French china dolls are Jumeau and Bru. Bru was in business from 1866, and is reckoned the better of the two. The Jumeau company, with a fairly obscure partner, Belton, was established in 1842, obtaining their heads from other companies but making their own from the 1860s There are various makers' marks, some of them confusing, as the retailer could also add their name, and the quality is variable. Depending on price costumes could be wool or a more expensive material, eyes

Below: A walking talking doll by Simon and Halbig, one of the many to try to create stability in a basically unstable structure. Until the coming of electronics talking was very much a minor art.

could be painted on or be of glass, and for almost the first time realistic bosoms were created for the more daring low-cut dresses. The doll-makers promoted their products diligently, creating room-like settings both in Paris and overseas to display the dolls at their best, and it is clear that adults rather than children were being targeted. These formidably clad lady dolls must have seemed alarming to many a young girl.

The child doll, the bébé, was invented with various doll-makers claiming that this was their invention. Children were encouraged to ask, even scream, for the bébé by parties organized for them, and competition among the children was actively encouraged. The sales catalogues of Jumeau constantly refer to the "beautiful French faces" of their child dolls, as opposed to, presumably, German faces. The Germans were increasingly in opposition, not only on the battlefield during the Franco-Prussian War (1870-1) but in the bazaars and arcades of Paris, and they would eventually win.

Bébés are amongst the most desirable of dolls for reasons which would not take a psychologist long to work out, and they came in an immense variety for the overseas market – negro, mulatto, Oriental, as well as standard white. The Japanese retaliated by producing their own Jumeau lookalikes and as marking was very haphazard these are going the rounds as genuine articles. In recent years genuine old Jumeau moulds have been discovered and have been put to good use.

Bru's bébés commonly represent a child of about four or between eight and eleven, with budding breasts with tinted nipples, and the hands were characteristically drooping. There were Brus where the chest moved up

Opposite: A fine leather-bodied high fashion doll with its extensive wardrobe. With increased competition, costume and accessories were made more elaborate and comprehensive.

Below: Bru was one of the great French doll makers, relatively unchallenged in its sphere until the arrival of the German dolls after the Franco-Prussian War. This one has a bisque head and swivels.

Left: A selection of various dolls, showing the great variety amongst even contemporary models.

and down as though breathing, and where the doll appeared to be drinking from a bottle (operated by turning a key in the back of the head). Between 1867 and 1869 Bru applied for many patents. The crying doll had a rubber ball placed inside the body fitted with a reed which made a crying sound; the double-faced Surprise Doll had a vertical rod in the interior which allowed the head to rotate without disarranging the doll's hair; a patent applied for in 1872 by Madame Bru was for another Surprise Doll; this one contained a tiny music box.

Bru also produced rubber dolls as no doubt the expensive china dolls had a short shelf life if actually played with, and he was also experimenting with realistically moving eyelids. Open and shut eyes were long used, activated by a lever, though the lead-weighted eyelids were introduced , becoming the standard method for opening and closing eyes. The advertisements have a note of hysteria , even though Bru was winning medals at the numerous international exhibitions. an In 1883 the firm passed to H. Chevrot, though the brand name was

Above: Dolls were divided into three categories: those modelled on adults, those on children, and those on babies ("bébés), the latter enjoying a vogue towards the end of the nineteenth century when cuteness and sentimentality were in fashion

Opposite: Three bisque swivel-headed French dolls, sometimes known as Parisiennes especially by modern doll dealers wishing to impart a cachet.

retained. Under Chevrot Bru pros-
pered, and although Bru himself
had won medals they were not gold;
Chevrot won gold medals. He and
his successor Girard were as innov-
ative as Bru himself, patenting
inventions for combined eye and
eyelid movement, and a walking
and talking doll, the Bébé Petit Pas.
Kissing dolls were patented in 1895
and 1897, but the clock was ticking
for French doll-making.

Jumeau was working on parallel
lines to Bru though he was not so
patent-crazy, and he too won
medals at exhibitions, with rather
more gold medals than Bru. As with
Bru, the German competition was
becoming too strong and Jumeau
sacrificed quality for quantity. In
1881 he made 85,000 bébés, in
1884 220,000, and was giving huge
discounts to retailers. In 1899
Jumeau and Bru merged with other
doll-making companies as a way of
countering the German makers, and
this combine, the Société Francaise
de Fabrication de Bébés et Jouets,
lasted until the inter-war period,
employing nearly 3,000 people. In
1912 the firm claimed to have produced five million dolls.

Jumeau and Bru bébés are often
similar, though Jumeau dolls are

more often marked. Jumeau child dolls had large liquid eyes set close
together, Bru dolls' eyes are set wider apart and give a startled expression. Bru dolls are generally heavier than those by Jumeau.

It is often supposed that the German doll-makers supplanted the
French because of their great gifts of organization and promotion,
and it is often overlooked that the porcelain industry in Germany
had been supreme in the eighteenth century, while in France innovation had been stifled by restrictions placed on porcelain factories
by the monarch, leaving only Sèvres, which was almost a monopoly, powerful enough to compete with dozens of German factories
in the various states. The French porcelain factories had a sense of
inferiority, and were forever apprehensive. There was also a psy-
chological dimension in that France had been defeated by Germany
in the Franco-Prussian War and suffered from a sense of inferiority.

Some of the German firms, such as Dressel, had a long history of
doll making in other media before venturing into bisque, but not
only did the Germans produce dolls of equal quality to the French
but they created new variations, evolving "character" dolls, in which

*Above: A somewhat elongated-faced bisque-
headed bébé made by the renowned French
firm of Jumeau, the main rival to Bru in the
prestige stakes.*

*Opposite: A porcelain-headed doll with
torso and limbs of kid displayed at the
Paris Exhibition of 1878 and therefore reckoned to be above the ordinary. Exhibitions
proliferated from 1851 onwards and served
as an important promotional technique for
the makers.*

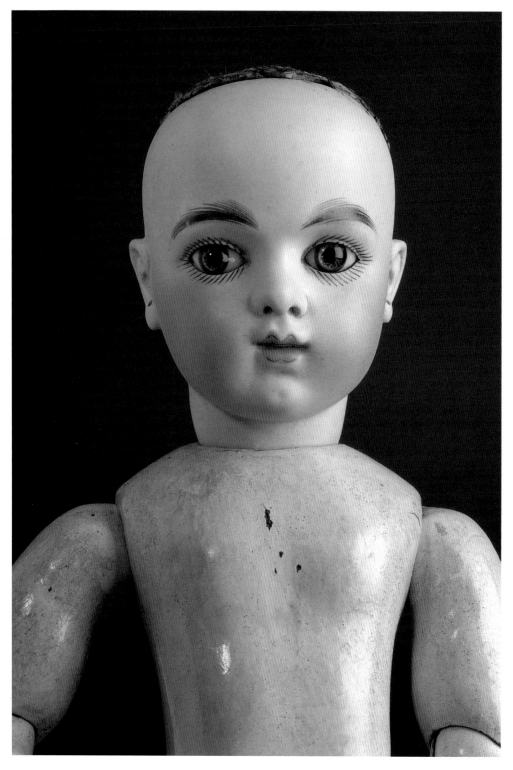

Above: Open-mouthed dolls were usually reckoned cuter, but this is a closed-mouth bisque headed bébé, generally less popular as a genre as the dolls could look sullen.

Opposite: Two bisque-headed dolls dressed in red and russet peasant coloured clothes of the period.

real children had real expressions, far removed from the static quality of the French bébés, and did real things (a whistling boy character doll actually whistled when his stomach was pressed).

These were much more demanding to make, necessitating the use of more moulds and a more sophisticated use of body-making materials, while some of them were crammed with gimmicks. The character doll was taken up in America, where it formed the basis of the massive American doll industry which, previously, had made little more impact than the British china doll trade.

The largest producer of dolls in Germany was Armand Marseille, who set up a company in Koppelsdorf in 1865. Other major doll-makers were J. D. Kestner (who probably pioneered fur eyebrows), the Heubach Brothers, Simon and Halbig, and Kammer and Reinhardt, and they exported widely to Britain and America as well as France, which copied them with a good deal of verve. Kammer and Reinhardt attempted to make a speaking doll with an Emil Berlin phonograph concealed in the body, but not surprisingly it failed. Heubach invented a walking doll activated by clockwork and mounted on three wheels. Something of an innovation was a doll in rabbit costume, with an egg container attached to the backs of their legs, presumably a one-off for Easter.

Except for the character dolls, the German makers took their tone from the French pioneers in bisqu. The quality was variable though the best were never, it is alleged, as good as the best French models, though it has been traditional to look down on them as there are so

many more on the market than French dolls. Nevertheless the most expensive doll sold at auction (so far) was made by Kammer and Reinhardt, selling for £190,000 at Sotheby's, London, in 1994.

A variation on character dolls was the Piano Baby, first made by Heubach, presumably designed as an ornament, which was made in some quantity and heralded a move towards cuteness and sentimentality, epitomised many years later in 1913 by the American "Kewpies" (from Cupid). Piano Babies usually come in pairs, with the eyes trained on each other, and are made in the form of infants crawling, seating, or lying on their backs. Most commonly they wore white chemises trimmed with pale pink blue or turquoise. Some Piano Babies wore large floppy bonnets.

Armand Marseile Junior visited America in 1904 to study American business methods, and the firm continued into the 1930s. Marseile dolls bore a mould mark (the most common is 390) and more Marseile dolls exist than those of any other named manufacturer. They are of widely varying quality depending on the target market. There was so much competition that profit margins were drastically reduced.

During World War I there was, of course, no export of German dolls to Britain from 1914 and America from 1917, and both countries began to make their own bisque dolls which were of modest quality. Exports were resumed after the war, but America had its own massive industry and whereas pre-war the Germans could undercut almost all nations, the financial chaos of the German monetary system made their products uncompetitive. The interest in china dolls was less, with composition and new materials taking the place of porcelain.

Above: Giving dolls names was accompanied by giving dolls character descriptions. "My dream baby" was made in the Oriental style by the German firm of Armand Marseille some time after 1924.

Opposite: A twentieth-century Japanese doll of little consequence, but made interesting by the paraphernalia surrounding her.

DOLLS' HOUSES

Strongly associated with dolls, and appealing to the same kind of collector, are dolls' houses, the first recorded example of which was made for Duke Albrecht of Bavaria's daughter in 1558. The craze spread like wild fire among the well-to-do. The Dutch were pre-eminent in this field, and their "cabinets" contained miniature furniture and effects, including tiny pieces of oriental porcelain and oil paintings in carved frames. The largest producer of miniatures to furnish and service a "baby house" as they

were called until the 1830s (though the phrase lingered on into the 1880s) was eventually Germany. The quintessential German classic was a kitchen, with everything beautifully made, including sides of bacon meticulously carved from wood. These were to instruct German girls in domestic science.

British and American dolls' houses were not so elegantly furnished as their Dutch contemporaries. However, what they lacked in style they gained in invention and eccentricity, and unlike the Dutch houses were often clearly intended for children rather than adults. Most dolls' houses were made to stand against a wall, though there are exceptions such as the Italian dolls' house of the seventeenth century which was meant to stand in the middle of the room so it could be viewed from all sides.

It was an astonishingly long-lived mania, and still survives, perhaps because it gives scope to the hobbyist who can not only make the house, possibly from cardboard, but personally create the contents, though there were dozens of firms providing miniature furniture. The well-off frequently created miniatures of their own houses, made by the estate carpenter, and no expense was spared. The most famous of all dolls' houses was made by the architect Sir Edwin

Above: Miniature furniture and dolls'-house equipment were preceded by model kitchenware, as in these fine Dutch examples, a silver jug of 1746, a silver cup of 1725 - 1750, a silver tea kettle 1725 - 1775, and a silver beaker of the same period. Unlike the British, the Dutch had no exact assay marks to give a precise year

Opposite: A dolls' house of the highest quality and rarity from about 1760, exceptionally elaborate and well-fitted. Doll's-house making eventually became a major do-it-yourself activity for better or for worse.

Overleaf: A six-roomed town dolls' house which may have been modelled on a house in Seymour Place, London, now 18 - 23 Curzon Street.

Previous page: The village school, a quaint set of felt dolls modelled by the famous maker Steiff about 1910. The move towards "ordinary-people" dolls was instigated in America, which towards the end of the nineteenth century was exporting its own dolls in quantity to the traditional doll-making countries of western Europe.

Right: A painted wooden grocer's shop.

Lutyens for Queen Mary, wife of King George V of England. This is more of an exquisite scale model than a dolls' house and was actually equipped with electricity, though it is rivalled by Titania's Palace, designed by Sir Nevile Wilkinson.

Perhaps the best known of American miniature houses (rather than a dolls' house) is Coleen Moore's display castle in the Museum of Science and Industry in Chicago which has a working organ and a drawing room with a jade and rose quartz floor.

Queen Victoria's dolls' house was fairly modest, with two rooms, a large kitchen downstairs and a drawing room above. Restraint was not a feature which lasted as the nineteenth century progressed. Dolls' houses became increasingly surreal and technologically advanced. Most manufactured dolls' houses are unmarked, though Lines Brothers were a major supplier, retailing their products through Gamages, the London department store and advertised in trade catalogues. A dolls' house of 1907, costing £25 – three months wages for the average worker – had a cistern in the roof space which supplied heated water. A dolls' house of 1910 had real fires in the grates which could be lit so that the smoke rose through the chimneys.

The eighteenth-century dolls' house was elegant in proportion and full of fine detail, usually made of wood and containing miniature silver and mahogany furniture as stylish and well-made as the full-grown article. Limoges enamels were often cannibalized to make pictures though it was more usual to use tiny prints. Although the use of wood persisted, the increasing market in the nineteenth century amongst the middle classes led to the widespread use of thick-gauge cardboard. This was often provided plain so that the owner could create the finish wanted using sheets of paper depicting bricks or other material.

The Americans imitated brownstone by sprinkling sand onto a glue-covered surface giving a sandpaper-like effect. One of the few known American makers was the R. Bliss Manufacturing Company of Rhode Island which used isinglass (mainly gelatine, originally made from sturgeons' air bladders) for the windows. In 1911 Bliss featured fold-up dolls' houses made of heavy board with cloth hinges; it was proudly proclaimed that they could be dismantled in less than a minute.

The structure of the house depended on the skill and imagination of the maker, or lack of it, so there are houses where staircases lead nowhere, rooms lack doors, and walls are without windows. Some of the rooms are impossible to see into. In most cases the front of the house is hinged to display the interior, though a few hinge from the side... The scale of the items is sometimes bizarre, depending on what was available. High-class miniature objects were imported from Germany, especially Augsburg, Ulm and Hesse Cassel and at the bottom of the market there was furniture cut out from card. Eighteenth-century dolls' houses were peopled with small wax or wooden figures, but when porcelain-headed dolls appeared in the nineteenth century these were used, often being too large for their surroundings, though scale was not a question which troubled many. In the late 1870s the commercial potential of a doll's-house family was seen especially in America and in 1913 the ultimate variety included "Gentlemen and Ladies in different costumes, Maids, Nurses, Waiters,

Above: A timber-framed dolls' house, commercially made by A. G. & J. Lines, model number 37, of painted wood and printed paper.

Opposite: A large wooden dolls' house with steps, made in what was considered the Spanish style, painted to resemble brick-work, though the sides are plain.

Butlers, Cooks, etc. These dolls measure from five to seven inches and range in price from 50c to $1.50." Obviously they were intended for larger-than-average dolls' houses, or perhaps not considering the eccentricities of many dolls'-house owners.

Sheets of miniature wallpaper were provided by the manufacturers, and owners of dolls' houses often kept up with fashion by repapering. Modern owners renovating old dolls' houses sometimes find that there are up to six layers of wallpaper. Carpets were usually paper, though hobbyists sometimes used chenille or velvet. Home-made houses are often very heavy, being made of thick wood. Plywood, the ideal material for twentieth-century dolls' houses was not evolved until 1917.

They are frequently inconsistent – a well-made door with brass

Previous pages right: A dolls' house. Children could customise their dolls' houses by sticking on lithographed pattern paper representing brickwork, stucco, or other finishes. Brownstone was especially popular in America.

Right: Unusually, this fine doll's house of about 1875 is fully furnished with its original furniture. The temptation amongst adult owners to up-date the decor is often overwhelming.

LOOK! ONLY 14 Cts for 3 French Dolls

WITH AN ELEGANT WARDROBE OF 32 PIECES.

CHRISTMAS IS COMING.

CHEAPEST and BEST.

Consisting of Reception, Evening and Morning Dresses, Bonnets, Street Costumes, Cloaks, Hats, Hand Satchels, Sun Umbrellas, Music Portfolios, Overcoats, Sailor Suits, Military Suits, Drums, Street Jackets, Watering Place Suits, Travelling Costumes, Dress Suits, &c. These Dresses and Suits in this Elegant Wardrobe represent Nine Different Colors, and they are lovely beyond description, several being from Designs by Worth, of Paris. There is One Little Boy and Two Girl Dolls in Each Set, with Pretty Faces and Life-like Beautiful Features, and their Wardrobe is so extensive that it takes hours to dress and undress them in their Different Suits. Every Child and every Mother that has seen them go in ecstacies over them. Children will get more real enjoyment out of a Set of these French Dolls than out of articles that cost $10. Every person that buys them sends immediately for more. A Lady writes us that her Little Boy and Girl played for five long hours with a Set of these French Dolls, and they felt very sorry indeed to think that they must stop and eat their supper, and if mothers only knew how much amusement there is in these Dolls they would willingly pay double the price asked for them. Sample set consisting of three dolls with their wardrobe of 32 pieces, by mail for 14 cents, 2 sets, 6 dolls, 64 pieces, for 22c., 12 sets for $1, you get $1.80; 25 sets for $2, you get $3.75 for them; 50 sets for $3.85, you get $7.50; 100 sets $6 by express, you get $15. Any boy, girl or agent can sell 100 sets every day; if you do that you make over $50 a week. If you send for one or two sets we will send our Secret Method and Full Directions how you can make more than $100 a month out of these dolls. You have not one day to lose, as each days' delay is dollars lost to you. If you have not the money now cut this out, as it will not appear again before Christmas, and is an opportunity too valuable to lose. Postage stamps taken. Address **M. BABCOCK & CO., CENTERBROOK, CONN.**

fittings contrasting with an otherwise unenterprising interior, though it is difficult to find a boring dolls' house, so manic was the desire to include everything including pets (the pug was the most popular dog).

The best furniture was made of rosewood and transfer printed with gold decorative detail, with drawers that opened and real-glass mirrors that tilted at a touch. It was quite cheap – whatnots cost sixpence (two and a half pence) and sideboards one and three (six pence). Cheaper furniture was made of pine and decorated with blue or red flowers and many kitchen dressers have survived. French dolls' houses were often elegant and incorporated balconies and imitation wrought-iron work. Cane was often used for the furniture, simulating bentwood.

The cleverness of some of the small furnishings of dolls' houses defies belief, tiny ivory opera glasses and complete dinner and tea services, mostly imported from Germany. The English manufacturers preferred the toy tea and dinner services, though miniature creamware was made in Leeds with food such as fish or vegetables moulded onto the plate. For Queen Mary's house Royal Doulton was commissioned to provide the pottery. But one senses that those who had the most enjoyment were those who used old chess men, cotton reels, beads, porcupine quills, and whatever was handy to create something to add to the invariable clutter. Few dolls' houses are chic or sparsely furnished, and although twentieth-century houses contain lavatories – often mysteriously missing from Victorian specimens – radios, and telephones, there is very little minimalism, and the Art Deco movement of the 1920s and 1930s seems to have bypassed most devotees.

DOLLS' HOUSES in great variety, with 2, 3, or 4 Rooms, from 3/6 to £10. 10s.

Left: Dolls' houses were often sold alongside model shops, zoos and menageries, and, as in this instance, stables, though of a rather odd and mysterious design.

Opposite: This dolls' house belonging to Queen Mary, wife of King George V, was made by Ascroits of Liverpool in 1920. Queen Mary's dolls' houses were of superb quality, furnished regardless of expense.

DOLLS AND BEARS

The early twentieth century was one of the most exciting periods in doll-making, and there was a feeling that the traditional bisque dolls, whether lady dolls or child dolls, had had their day and it was time for something new and, in America, stimulating and suitable for aggressive advertising. This was led by character dolls in bisque, and it became clear to the manufacturers that the public was looking for the out of the ordinary, even the quirkish. Bisque manufacturers continued to ply their trade successfully because there was always an old-fashioned demand for the traditional and the pretty-pretty, and the Bye-Lo doll, with the head made in Germany and the remainder in America, was a runaway success in 1924 and extensively copied.

Children in particular preferred the undemanding insipidity provided by many of the German makers, who, as ever, had a firm grip of public taste. Some bisque models had enormous success such as the Mein Liebling Kammer and Reinhardt doll of about 1911, and the American and German Kewpie dolls of 1913.

A sign of the future was the success of the American commercially produced muslin-faced rag doll produced in the closing years of the nineteenth century, and there was a shift of emphasis from rag dolls for the poor to rag dolls for everyone. They were now more inclined to be called fabric dolls, and velvet, cloth and especially felt was used. Although the golden age of the fabric doll was probably 1910 – 1935, they had been successfully produced in the nine-

Above: After World War I the market in fine bisque or china dolls declined, but novelty dolls continued to make their appearance.

Opposite: The cheap doll market welcomed the introduction of celluloid and plastic, and many dolls were based on well-known film stars such as Shirley Temple.

Right: In this advertisement of the late 1880s, the letters of recommendation by titled ladies are of more interest than the doll, Miss Dollie Daisie Dimple, with her "trunk of smart clothes".

Opposite: Glove puppets have a long ancestry in Britain and Europe, Punch and Judy being the most illustrious, and have always enjoyed a vogue, especially since television made them popular, if hardly an art form.

Overleaf: Fabric dolls made in Pakistan for the home market. All societies have always made their own dolls, often by outworkers, often by poor mothers. Some of the existing dolls of the past have replacement faces, the originals having worn out.

teenth century for a largely undemanding market with little fuss and promotion.

Although humour had been present in the bisque character dolls fabrics were more suitable for the comic and the eccentric. Amongst the leaders was the German firm of Steiff, best known for their Teddy Bears, which claimed that it was the first to make fabric toys, a strange claim. Certainly it may have been the first to make fabric toys on a mass-production basis in Germany. By 1908 Steiff employed 2,000 workers. Margarette Steiff, the founder of the firm, claimed that she herself personally checked every doll. She had first begun by using scraps of felt supplied by a nearby factory, and her dolls are typified by a central seam running down the faces and black button eyes. In 1905 she introduced a distinctive trade mark, the knopf imm ohr (button in the ear), but these were often taken out by parents in the belief that the children would take them out and swallow them. The button-in-the-ear trademark is one of the distinguishing features of Steiff Teddy Bears which make them very expensive when they come up for sale.

The variety was immense, and many of the figures slyly mocked the establishment, with pompous officials portrayed in comic form, dwarfs, ethnic characters of all kinds including archetypal Irishmen and lederhosen-clad Germans. The appeal was robust and amiable both to the Germans and to the overseas market, and Steiff continues today to make these attractive figures. They were a breath of fresh air into what had become a staid industry. Margarete Steiff died in 1909

and the firm was taken over by her nephews.

Another German manufacturer was Käthe Kruse who made fabric dolls for her own children, collaborated with other doll-makers, and then started her own company in 1910, using wadded calico, though an interesting innovation was filling the schenkerle or Sand Baby with sand. These were so convincing that many were bought by maternity hospitals to help nurses give young mothers the feel of a real baby. The Bambino is also unusual in that it is tiny and made to be a doll's own doll. The Kruse dolls were all made by hand and were consequently expensive.

In the 1920s another German firm, Schuco, began making soft dolls and toys. These often had a clockwork mechanism or a wire link between the head and the tail which turned the head when the

Above: Anything connected with British royalty is inevitably immediately translated into dolls and toys. The Coronation in 1953 of Queen Elizabeth II was a case in point, especially as it was the first major occasion to have mass television coverage in Britain.

Opposite: A rare jester Teddy bear. These are often less rated by the true collectors than the standard cuddly version, but manufacturers mistakenly believe that novelty is everything.

Above: A selection of dolls, toys, with a Teddy bear from Victorian and Edwardian times, set incongruously against a fireplace as though due for ritual burning.

Previous page: Four mechanical dolls, two with pushers, two on cycles.

Opposite: An all-composition American doll, "Anne Shirley", from 1936, when conventional doll making was in a trough.

tail was turned. Schuco are probably best remembered for pioneer remote-controlled model cars which were ahead of anything else produced at the time.

Few American dolls were made commercially until after the Civil War. The first bisque doll was not manufactured until shortly before World War I, though the Americans experimented greatly in the late nineteenth century in composition and steel dolls. Aluminium dolls were first made in 1898 and they continued to be mnufactured until the early 1920s when they fell out of fashion. All-steel dolls were made from 1903 using thin sheet steel with steel springs.

The great cities of the east were as sophisticated as those in Europe,

but for those opening up the west the rag doll and the wood doll were the standard dolls. Izannah Walker of Central Falls registered a patent for stockinette rag dolls 1873; she made her dolls' heads by pressing together layers of glue-soaked cloth in moulds, adding a soft padding layer, and then putting on the stockinette which is a woven elasticated material of silk or wool.

There was a great interest in making unbreakable dolls, especially in America, and celluloid was the chosen medium. One of the celluloid dolls " is the merriest little fellow in toyland. Sells at sight. Can't Break Em art head and jointed pink or white velvet bodies'. They were widely sold in England advertised as "twelve inches of sunshine for 5/- (25p). 300,000 sold in four months. A combination of the character doll and the Teddy Bear." About the same time came "the jointed Boo Boo doll. The only naturally shaped baby doll made. Although only produced a few months ago thousands have been sold. 45/- (£2.25) or 36/- (£1.80) a dozen." The American doll had arrived in England along with the aggressive advertising.

JOINTED
Cloth Doll.

Patented.

Price on one-half yard of cloth,

10 cents.
For Sale by Your Dealer.

If he has not got them show him this advertisement and he will get it for you.

Do not send to us as we have none at retail.

See full page in COMPANION PREMIUM LIST for "Tabby Cat," "Pug Dog," "Skye Terrier," "Rabbit," "Monkey," "Owl," "Little Red Riding Hood," and "Negro Dollie."

Arnold Print Works,

Left: For ten cents one gets what one pays for, and one dreads what the "Companion Premium List" offers. It is interesting that what is "dolly" in Britain (a familiar form of Dorothy) is "dollie" in America.

Below: A late nineteenth-century advertisement for two dolls, a soldier doll, and a jointed doll of repellent aspect dressed in velvet and fur.

CATALOGUE POST FREE.

SOLDIER DOLLS, dressed as Grenadier, Hussar, Naval Officer, Black Watch, & several other patterns at 10/6 each.

JOINTED DOLL, dressed in velvet, trimmed fur, hand made clothes, to undress. Prices, 18/6, 21/-, 25/-, 28/-, 32/6, to 63/-.

Opposite: Despite the state's renown in fine and applied arts, Italian dolls are little known, and this 1920s boy and girl by the firm of Lenci are somewhat uncommon

One of the problems of advertising is to come up with an appealing name, and this was especially true of American dolls. Some are so strange that one wonders how they came into being. The Aceedeecee doll of 1920 when spoken aloud gives AC/DC, and possibly gave an unfortunate child an electric shock! More conventional names were Adèle (1886), Adeline (1916), Alice Lee (1924), and the rather flatly named American Doll (1919-1921), American Fashion (1905) and the

American Girl (1907-12). Between 1911 and 1921 there was a range of dolls called American Kids in Toyland.

Many dolls had boys' or girls' names, others described their costume such as Arctic Boy of 1913, others were comical, such as Andy Gump of 1924, based on a comic-strip character of the time, but amongst the leaders were cute names such as Dolly Winkle (1918-1919), and the Dollypop Dolls of 1925. Dolly Dumplings of 1918 was a good line with more than two hundred different models. Amongst the most interesting are the character dolls based on people who enjoyed a vogue and then disappeared into oblivion such as Dorothy Stone who played Peter Pan in some long-forgotten production in about 1924.

Another unbreakable material was rubber, used throughout the nineteenth century but not extensively. The rubber hardened and cracked within a fairly short time. A different kind of rubber was

Above: A selection of Steiff Teddy bears doing a jigsaw puzzle, a highly marketable combination (jigsaws were enormously popular during the 1920s and 1930s).

Opposite: A Steiff monkey of about 1910. Unlike the celebrated Teddy bear, other Steiff animal toys failed to make an impact, though it was in America and Britain only that the Steiff bear became a cult, now so expensive as to be out reach of those on a modest budget.

Left: Cattley family toys from about 1906.

developed, and the Americans introduced the rubber Drydee Baby which "drank" from a bottle and appeared to wet its nappy when a plug was removed from its bottom. Novelty was all. Some dolls were giveaways with coupons from the sale of soap and other everyday commodities. The most indestructible material was of course wood, and the Americans re-introduced wood dolls, such as the All Wood Perfection Art Dolls, painted in washable enamel colours and dressed in simple clothes. The dolls were jointed by an ingenious system of springs and could be posed in any position. The problem of making a life-like body was almost solved.

Celluloid was invented in the nineteenth century and consisted of soluble cellulose, nitrate, and camphor, a viable material when new but it was soon subject to discolouring and it looked cheap. It was also highly inflammable. Heads were made by blowing steam or hot air into moulds. Pioneers in this technique were the Hyatt Brothers who

Opposite: Cut-out dolls and dolls' clothes, including clothing for 1920s flappers and a clown. These cut-outs were often included in women's magazines, though they were of course sold separately. With just two shoulder tabs to press down they were hardly demanding, unlike the effort that had to be put in to dress Victorian dolls

Overleaf: Four fine Teddy bears from Germany, made in 1910 from Yorkshire cloth.

Above: A corn husk folk doll of late Victorian times, surprisingly well dressed considering the crudity of the doll and its voodoo-like appearance.

Opposite: A bisque-headed bébé with walking legs and a voice box. The voice box was a later development of the "squeaker" as used not only in dolls but many animal soft toys, and some achieved a degree of sophistication and comprehension.

worked under the trade name of the Celluloid Novelty Company, but the best of the celluloid dolls were made in Germany from the 1870s, the models being bisque heads. As they were more expensive than bisque their popularity was limited. In 1903 a method of coating celluloid with bisque was used to imitate wax. Celluloid was used until World War I (when Japanese celluloid dolls were imported) but after the war it gradually lost favour except for the very cheapest dolls.

The American material Biskoline was similar to celluloid except, the makers claimed, it would "never break, crack, surface chip or peel". Another composition was Adtocolite, which cracked very badly and was a short-lived product but the perfect material was hard to find, and many compositions were patented, some of them hardly different from traditional papier mâché, though in one stone is one of the constituents. In the 1920s a concept by the Americans in the 1900s, the art doll, reached its fruition in a country not noted for its doll-making expertise, Italy, which is rather surprising as along with other Catholic countries Italy was adept at producing religious crèche dolls. The art doll was intended to be not only a plaything but a fashion accessory for women, and the leader in this field was the firm of Lenci. They have pressed felt faces, and are of the highest quality, are normally in the form of small children, but there were also golfing figures and tennis figures complete with golf bags and tennis rackets, as well as images of real people, such as the film star Rudolph Valentino.

Lenci was in tune with the times as one of the dolls is a young boy dressed somewhat clumsily in a Fascist uniform. Lenci figures were much copied, though the standard of the genuine article deteriorated during the Depression.

Since the age of wax dolls the British had been at the periphery of the doll world, but in the 1920s their fabric dolls were the equal of any in the world and superior to most of them, largely thanks to the Chad

Previous pages left: An intricately constructed clown violinist. Such objects were much more than mere dolls.

Previous pages right: A clockwork automaton modelled as a clown, a popular subject.

Right: Chad Valley was one of the most important British toy makers, responsible for a vast range of products, many of them adventurous and clever, and this felt-headed set of Snow White dolls and associated dwarfs capitalised on the first Disney full-length cartoon.

Right: This clockwork automaton of a white rabbit in a lettuce was not a plaything. The line between mechanical toys and automata is very fine.

Opposite: A selection of Action Men, one of the first to cash on television-type heroes, a continuation of the Superman tradition of the 1930s which resulted in many toys and accessories, much to the disgruntlement of adults as a key weapon was a water-pistol.

Overleaf: A small Negro playing a banjo, a quality French automaton produced towards the end of the nineteenth century.

Valley company of Birmingham, started in 1823 as a printing and bookbinding firm under the name of Johnson Brothers. Chad Valley was registered in 1919, named after the nearby River Chad. Chad Valley, who made a vast range of toys, specialised in felt and velvet dolls with a topical flavour including Bonzo the dog (1920), Mabel Lucie Attwell dolls, the young princesses Elizabeth and Margaret, and film stars such as Shirley Temple. As a surprisingly large number of nineteenth and twentieth-century doll-makers were women, they had a shrewd idea of what would appeal to children and what would be a waste of time. Men had their own ideas; Scott of the Antarctic was

hardly a best-seller by any standards, though military figures were a popular line during World War I.

Norah Wellings was a Chad Valley employee but left and set up her own company, patenting heads finished with waterproof coating so that they could be washed. She found a distinctive niche by providing dolls to the transatlantic liners where they were sold as souvenirs. She also made children from a variety of foreign lands, a long-established way of obtaining exports.

The English firm of Merrythought found fame in 1930, Pedigree in 1942, and there was far more care in definitively labelling the products. Many dolls had squeakers in the body, activated by pressing the stomach. There were many ways to stuff the soft toys, with kapok and similar materials gaining ground over granulated cork, sawdust, and excelsior (fine wood shavings). Kapok is often believed to be a modern substance but its use dates back to 1750, and is cotton wool, sometimes termed silk cotton, and it is odd that early doll-makers did not turn to this.

A curious side line was produced by Dean's Rag Book Co. Ltd., founded in 1905; they produced calico sheets on which were designs to be cut out with scissors to make rag dolls. The company also made complete dolls including outstanding Mickey and Minnie Mouses in the 1930s. Cut-out calico was a development of the cut-out card doll, which had a long ancestry, developed from the superb-quality fashion plates in French illustrated magazines from the early nineteenth century. Paper figures dressed in a shift or petticoat were printed together with a range of interchangeable clothes. Among the first to see the potential was S. and J. Fuller of the charmingly named The Temple of Fancy, Rathbone Place, London. One of the first figures the firm produced was the Protean Figure of Metamorphic Costumes of 1810, costing a guinea (much more than a working man's weekly wage), There were twelve different outfits with 90 different articles of dress. The costumes ranged from a monk's habit to a German Hussar's uniform. Ackerman of London, a pioneer producer of lithographs, made in 1830 a boxed set of cut-outs, La Poupée Modèle. Throughout the 1920s and 1930s cut-out dolls were a standard feature of many women's and children's magazines, and they are a sure guide to the fashions of the time. Not surprisingly, few have survived.

Most doll designers are anonymous but Dean's recruited well-known artists such as Cecil Aldin and John Hassall and like Chad Valley ventured into film cartoon characters such as Popeye and Mickey Mouse. The line between dolls and soft toys was very narrow, and some doll-makers were making as many stuffed animals as dolls, a legacy of the invention of the Teddy Bear, and the anthropomorphic animals in cartoons from Felix the cat onwards on film and cartoon strips in newspapers featuring such characters as Rupert Bear fostered the demand. The provision of doll-like toys for young boys over the centuries has never been fully researched, and clearly the Teddy Bear was not the first stuffed toy to be acceptable to boys as well as girls, though when boys were dressed in skirts as a matter of course the ownership of a doll would have been acceptable, both to them and their peers.

Portrait dolls have been a feature of the doll scene since the eighteenth century, and one wonders at times who they were intended for.

Opposite: A bisque-headed bébé wearing a red silk and straw hat.

Dressel of Germany, the oldest doll firm recorded, produced in about 1900 composition dolls of President McKinley, Admiral Dewey, and Admiral Sampson. The McKinley doll had a short career, as the president was assassinated in 1901.

Talking dolls did not progress very much until the electronic age. Bellows had been used to produce sounds at an early period in doll manufacture, and Jumeau experimented using two strings, and this method was popular until World War I. Despite all the problems, phonograph and gramophone dolls were persisted with. One doll said one word when one leg was raised, and another when the process was carried out on the other. A French patent for moving lips was applied for as early as 1890, but although the ideas were there in abundance the technology was not, and "Mama" and "Papa" were the most the majority of dolls could accomplish. In 1924 the magazine Playthings announced that a French doll would shout when it was picked up, said four words, and sang a bit of a French song.

The walking doll was a concept long cherished. When skirts were long it was a simple matter to conceal wheels operated by a simple clockwork motor, but the swinging legs dolls of 1918–1922 provided more of a problem and there is doubt whether they could "walk" in the accepted sense of the word. They certainly could not walk unaided. The first true walking doll was the Autoperipatetikos of 1862, and the clockwork motor shuttled two large feet backwards and forwards below a flat base plate, technology well ahead of its time in terms of dolls but elementary in terms of the magnificent engineering of the Victorian age. Naturally all this mechanism was hidden by a long skirt.

After World War I fabric and bisque dolls were obliged to compete with dolls made from a new range of composition materials which could be coloured during the manufacturing process and which were soft and pliable to the touch, in other words squashable and therefore very appealing to young children. These were cheap to make and for the first time reasonable-quality dolls were available to the very poor, and even those dolls at the bottom of the market were fitted out with opening and closing eyes, usually using the lead-weighted eyelids method. Most were insipid, but this is what was wanted by the mass of the people, and as with fabric toys some were based on film stars such as Shirley Temple, the icon of the 1930s, even if they were minor variations on the basic chubby doll. Generally they were socketed, with bent legs and arms.

Childrens' choices were now more important than in the past, and through strenuous promotion and from the 1950s through television advertisements children were relentlessly targeted with new products, the most famous being the Barbie doll, its contemporaries and its copiers, and its accessories, remodelled at regular intervals and brought up to date with dozens of changes of clothing. Similar in background but hardly in the category of dolls was Action Man of the 1960s, with the manufacturers cashing in on a host of accessories.

It is a far cry from the exquisite wax dolls of the eighteenth century and later, even more from the Parisiennes, nor can there be a comparison with the enchanting fabric dolls of the 1920s and 1930s. No doubt the children then had to ask for their favourite dolls rather than demand them.

INDEX

PICTURE CREDITS